# Romanticizing the SIN NATURE

## Our Tendency Toward It, Our Call to Overcome It!

# JESUS MATEO

Romanticizing the Sin Nature
*Our Tendency Toward It, Our Call To Overcome It!*

Jesus Mateo
jmateo1774@gmail.com

ISBN 978-1-943342-20-4

Printed in the USA.
All rights reserved

Published by: Destined To Publish | Flossmoor, Illinois
www.DestinedToPublish.com

# DEDICATION

I would like to dedicate this book to my children, my mother, my brothers and sister, my extended family, my friends and acquaintances, and anyone who has struggled with their own sin nature.

May the Lord Jesus Christ open the eyes of your understanding to the power He makes available to you if you are truly in Him.

# ACKNOWLEDGMENTS

I am very thankful for the men and women of God who have had a hand in my spiritual development throughout the years. Without them, I could not have reached a point in life where I could even attempt to write a book on these things.

I would like to thank God for His grace which strengthened me throughout this writing process.

Thank you to my wife, Darcy, for her encouragement and input as I worked on this book.

Thank you to the very special people at Destined to Publish, Marilyn Alexander, Kara Bickhem May, and Deborah Anthony. Their guidance and feedback were invaluable.

# CONTENTS

# INTRODUCTION

Have you ever found yourself thinking life is moving way too fast? Maybe you are thinking there are not enough hours in the day to accomplish everything you'd like to. Sometimes it can feel like we are sleepwalking through life or just running on a hamster wheel: lots of activity but going nowhere. Have you ever felt that way about your spiritual life? I have, and it was an uncomfortable realization – uncomfortable because I knew I could not continue living life this way.

What if I told you there is a power play happening in your life, whether you are aware of it or not? The Bible teaches us that there is only one God we should serve, but there are many things that want to occupy the position of master in your life. In this book, I would like to spotlight sin (the breaking of God's law) as one of these forces looking to be master over your life. I have had a chance to see just how much people are okay with living outside of what we know to be a righteous life and expecting things to turn out all right for them. Their sin has become master over them, and their thoughts and actions are now being controlled.

What's worse is, many times, the way we are living is exactly where we want to be, if we are being honest. Many openly welcome sin to run things because it is what they desire. We live double lives, one way in one place and a different way in another. This can be viewed as having a love affair with sin. It is like entering into an intimate relationship with your worst enemy. It is romanticizing sin. God has called us to live holy, righteous lives, so you cannot expect this kind of thing to go on without seeing the consequences of those actions. In Christ, we are free from slavery to sin, so there is no excuse for sin being in charge in your life. God has called us to greater things, so we can't be content to stay in this condition. You must overcome any and all sins in your life and then maintain mastery over them.

So, how is this done? How can I jump off the hamster wheel and do great things? How can I live a life that honors God and fulfills His purposes for me? Thankfully, God gives us the answers in His Word.

My prayer is that as you read through this book, you will find what God is trying to say to you, and you will find encouragement to rule over sin in your life and not allow it to rule you.

# Ignorance, Self-Deception, or Disobedience?

Have you ever experienced betrayal? It hurts to know someone you trusted has stabbed you in the back, doesn't it? You may have been blinded by what you thought was a friendship, partnership, or love, when in reality, that person never had your best interest at heart. They were setting you up the whole time, and you couldn't even see it. Even if a real friend tried to warn you, you were too blind to see all the red flags.

There's a saying, "Hindsight is 20/20," meaning that we often have the full knowledge and complete understanding of an event only after it has happened. Unfortunately, finding out your enemy's plans only after they have completed them doesn't do you much good. At best, it can be something you learn from and hopefully never allow to happen again. Would you fall for it if you knew your enemy's plans from the beginning? I think I can confidently say you would have no part in your enemy's schemes for you. It would seem crazy if you knew the intention of the person who wanted to wrong you and still decided to allow yourself to be vulnerable. Well, I want to tell you that, spiritually, most if not all of us have done just that.

What is sin, exactly? Sin is described in the Bible as a transgression of God's law or rebellion against Him. We see sin enter into humanity in the book of Genesis through the devil's temptation of Adam and Eve. As soon as they broke God's commandment (do not eat of the tree of the knowledge of good and evil), the pure nature died and the sin nature entered.

There is a progression that happens with sin. First it begins in the mind as a thought, then it progresses to be a desire, and finally it manifests as an action. You can't give sin an inch, because that's all the room it needs to infect us and start us down that slippery slope into more and more sin. It will build up into what the Bible describes as a stronghold. A stronghold can be defined as a place where a cause or a belief is strongly defended. That's why the more you engage in sin, the harder it is to break free from it. In order to fight sin, you will need more than willpower: you will need the power of God. *"For the weapons of our warfare are not carnal but mighty in God for pulling down strongholds, casting down arguments and every high thing that exalts itself against the knowledge of God, bringing every thought into captivity to the obedience of Christ"* (2 Corinthians 10:4-6 NKJV).

The sin nature in us desires to break God's commands and rebel against Him. When we sin against God, we allow for all types of trouble to come in and cause us harm. There is a great example of this in scripture. In Genesis 4:7, God speaks to Cain about how sin was trying to take control of his life. Here's how it reads in the New King James Version: *"If you do well, will you not be accepted? And if you do not do well, sin lies at your door. And its desire is for you, but you should rule over it."*

See, sin desires to take control of your life and run you. All you need to do is look at the things people struggle with, and you will see the sin that leads them around like a slave in bondage. Someone who struggles with pornography, fornication, or adultery is led by their lusts. Sin is never satisfied; it will only want more. It may start off small, but it will require more from you each time you go back to it. What's tragic is that people can even believe that it's what

3

they really want and that they are calling the shots, but it's their sin nature that's in control.

I have found in my own life that I fell into one of two categories when it came to the revelation of this scripture. I was unaware of just how prone my flesh was to the draw of sin (ignorance), or I was fooling myself into accepting that somehow sin wasn't that big a deal (self-deception). Falling into sin's trap out of ignorance can easily happen when you are new in your walk with Christ because you don't have understanding yet. It also happens when we allow ourselves to be biblically illiterate. This must be the worst possible position to put yourself in. We cannot rely solely on sermons or podcasts to be our only source of biblical knowledge. Always have a foundation of biblical knowledge built by reading the Word of God for yourself and asking the Holy Spirit to give you insight into what you are reading.

Some feel that once you say a few words accepting Christ as your Savior, you can then continue to live life as you previously did. But when you don't know and understand the Word of God, you fall into sin's traps out of ignorance. If Genesis 4:7 is new to you, then I suggest you take this passage of scripture very seriously now that you do know it. Once God gives us insight into His Word He expects for us to apply it to our lives. It is a serious thing, James 4:17 (NKJV) "Therefore, to him who knows to do good and does not do it, to him it is sin". This was a warning to Cain and also to the rest of us. Sin does not mean you any good.

Romans 6:23a (NKJV) reads, *"For the wages of sin is death"* – the payment you receive for serving sin is death. It is no friend of yours, so do not treat it like it is. Those of us who say that we serve Jesus Christ, that we are "Christians," should know this scripture and understand it. Sadly, in practice, we observe the opposite. If you know the scripture and understand it, then why would you entertain sin? If you open the door to sin and you know these things, you are living in self-deception or in outright disobedience. Any reason you can come up with for allowing sin to come in and control you is a lie you have accepted. The difference between self-deception and disobedience is that with self-deception, you are playing games with yourself and pretending that the sin you are in is somehow okay, while disobedience is simply knowing God's Word and doing what you want instead.

There was an instance where we were doing a Bible lesson with our kids on the topic of breaking free from sinful behavior. We had gone over things like this before with them, but this time I noticed something. There were things they easily and boldly rejected, but there were certain things that they were not so eager to renounce in their lives. I got a picture of how they were coddling these specific sins, romanticizing them instead of renouncing them. I believe God showed this to me not just for them, but also for myself and you. As I thought more about it, God showed me that just as the kids were struggling with certain things, so was I. I looked over my life and saw so many instances where instead of mastering sin, I allowed myself to be mastered by it.

There was a time when I was serving overseas in the Army, and several of us were tasked with working out at a remote helipad. On certain Saturdays, only one of us needed to be there, so we rotated those days. It was my turn on that particular Saturday, so I got into our work truck and started heading toward the helipad. The truck we were given to use was very run down and often stalled on us, but it was what we had to use. After the workday was done, it was dark and I was tired, I just wanted to get back to our barracks, and of course, this truck would not start no matter what I did. I felt my patience running thin and my temper rising at this junky truck. I finally lost my temper, and out of frustration, I hit the windshield with my hand. I didn't really think I struck it that hard, but now the windshield had a big crack in it.

I just remember feeling so foolish for letting my temper get the best of me. That was me allowing my anger to master me in that moment. Had I coddled that sin and kept it close to me, that sin would have ruined my life, as it would have progressed to more violent acts. I had friends and acquaintances who struggled with this and got themselves in bad situations because of it. It was their sin nature compelling them, and they had given into it to serve their anger and rage instead of dealing with the root issues. This is like an abusive relationship that we choose to return to: even though we were hurt before, we find ourselves going back. This abuser is looking for any way to gain entrance and ruin our lives.

As I researched this, I saw this parallel, and I looked at reasons why people stay in abusive relationships. While there were many reasons listed, I saw two that stuck out to me. The first one was speaking about normalized abuse. This is when someone grows up in an environment where abuse was common, so they accept their partner's behavior as normal. Spiritually, the same can be true. Too many people who claim to be believers in Christ practice sin openly. We tell our youth to keep themselves for marriage, but it is common for them to see "Christians" living together with their boyfriends or girlfriends.

I once heard an evangelist give an account of an event he did at a university, and he remembered this young man who came to Christ during the event. The young man stuck around to speak with this evangelist and let him know that he had been a Muslim and was compelled to attend the outreach event. Apparently, the Lord had been working on him for a while until he finally decided to attend this event.

The young, now ex-Muslim man wanted to ask so many questions about what he needed to do now and how to live his new life in Christ. To this, the evangelist said, "Find a local church or other Christians who attend the university with you to help guide you." The young man asked, "Do you mean like my roommate who routinely sleeps with his girlfriend? Is that who I'm supposed to go to for guidance?" The evangelist asked some follow-up questions about this young man's roommate, and apparently, he would claim that he was a Christian and was trying to tell him about Jesus, but it was difficult for the young man to receive anything his roommate and others had to say because their life didn't match their talk. Our youth are looking for people with conviction who not only tell them what is right but also live it. We will quickly tell our kids to watch their language, but when we are around certain people, we curse or tell crude jokes. In that kind of environment, it seems abuse is inevitable.

The other reason why people stay in abusive relationships is dependence on the abuser. This is where the abuser makes it so that the person being abused has few to no options for self-sufficiency. Sin can be a lot like an addiction – we all have a "God-shaped hole" in us, and trying to fill that void with sin (or anything else) is pointless. There is nothing that can take the place of God; any counterfeits will not be enough, so you try to use more and more to fill it, but it will never be enough. Once an addiction gets a hold on you, it is difficult to get rid of it. You start to desire that addiction more and more, and the next thing you know, you are dependent on it. So, you continue to return to this abuser called sin. When we allow ourselves to be drawn away by our desires, there is sin, waiting for us to open the door and pounce.

The Bible teaches that when Adam and Eve fell, we all inherited the sin nature. This means we all have our struggles, and no one is perfect. That is why no one can say this scripture does not apply to them. 1 John 1:8 (ESV) reads, *"If we say we have no sin, we deceive ourselves, and the truth is not in us."* The fact is, sin is at your door. In some translations, it says that sin is crouching at your door, ready to pounce on you. God's expectation is that we master it and not the other way around.

Recognizing that there is sin at your door is the first step. Just as God showed Cain the potential consequences of giving in to his sin, He is now showing you the same thing. As Cain allowed sin to take control, murderous thoughts started creeping into his mind, and eventually, he was mastered by his sin and did a terrible thing by killing his own brother. Once God brought light to Cain's sin, he had no excuse for allowing it to rule him. He was shown his would-be oppressor, and he chose to bow down to it. This was the first instance recorded of the struggle Man has inherited through the sin nature. We all have the same common enemies to contend with: the influences of this world, this flesh (sin nature) we live in, and yes, the devil. While I have been quick to blame the world around me for my mistakes or say the devil made me do it, the more accurate reason is that I did not exercise self-discipline. It is a struggle from all angles, but God is looking for us to overcome. So, how do we get there? Let's start by taking responsibility.

# Chapter 1 Devotional

## Scripture

James 1:21-22 (NKJV)

*"Therefore lay aside all filthiness and overflow of wickedness, and receive with meekness the implanted word, which is able to save your souls. But be doers of the word, and not hearers only, deceiving yourselves."*

## Devotional

The word of God goes out in different ways – maybe you've heard God's word through the radio, by speaking with a friend, or by attending a church service. God sent His word out in all sorts of ways in order to reach you and me. God's word reached me on a Chicago street corner as I was walking home from a friend's house one day, which led to my salvation. In this scripture, James, the half-brother of Jesus, is telling us that it's not enough to simply hear God's word: we must live it as well. If we don't live it, we are only fooling ourselves, because results come from applying God's word to your life. Applying God's word and living in it daily is where true change begins!

## QUESTIONS

Have you heard God's word lately? If so, what is God speaking to you? What is God trying to show you?

_____

_____

_____

_____

What can you do to apply what you've learned from God's word to your life today?

_____

_____

_____

*Take time to meditate on the words God has spoken to you, no matter how you received it, and ask Him to give you understanding of His word.

# TAKING RESPONSIBILITY

I read about a woman in Florida who went on a killing spree with her boyfriend. The boyfriend took his own life in a standoff with police, but the woman surrendered to the authorities. This woman claimed that her abusive boyfriend forced her to help commit the crimes, but when the authorities investigated, they saw she had done things like purchase ammunition on her own. The question that came up in her case was whether she was a victim or an accomplice.

On the one hand, she was with a very violent person who could have killed her at any time, but then there was evidence that she actively participated in the crime spree. The investigators concluded that there must have been a deeper connection than just fear keeping her with her boyfriend throughout the killing spree. In other words, they were saying she had the opportunity to flee and never took it. They were making the case that she was willing and therefore an accomplice, not a victim.

I do not know all the details of that case, but from what was disclosed, the evidence is stacked against her. In the same way, the evidence is stacked against us when it comes to our relationship with sin. Since I brought up a court case here, I think this is a good place to show how the enemy of your soul stands before God to accuse you continuously. Yes, the same enemy that is at work to influence you to commit sin is the one that turns around to accuse you before God. He goes to God to say, "Look, isn't he supposed to be your servant? He is out here doing those things you commanded him not to do." "He deserves to be punished; he deserves death!"

In times past, you would have had no advocate standing up for you, but thank God for His Son Jesus Christ who frees us. When the devil shows up with those accusations, your advocate is there to say, "It has been paid for." What an amazing God we serve! If you do not comprehend the high price that was paid for your sin that was too costly for you to pay, then you won't understand why you simply cannot continue to live a habitually sinful life. When we romanticize sin, we act as the accomplice to its destructive nature and the devil that accuses us, but we are also the victim, since we end up reaping the consequences of bad decisions.

There is a very key issue in Genesis 4:7b that we miss, either unintentionally or intentionally. The full scripture reads, *"If you do well, will you not be accepted? And if you do not do well, sin lies at the door"* (NKJV, emphasis added). This implies that we are responsible for our actions. However, we prefer to shift the blame whenever possible rather than accept responsibility. If we back up a little in scripture to Genesis 3, we find Adam and Eve looking to shift the blame to anybody other than themselves for their disobedience to God. Adam blamed Eve, and Eve blamed the serpent. Many times, people do not want to hear that they might have to own up to their mistakes and take responsibility for their actions. It's so much easier to say that you were the victim somehow, even though that was not the case. We would prefer to say that sin broke down our doors and made us do wrong, but of course we know this isn't true.

I remember as a young teen, I got a job working at a flea market selling clothes. The man who hired me didn't really pay much, but I was happy to have a job. Then I started to hear the complaining of the other workers, and suddenly greed started to be stirred up in me. I now felt I wasn't being compensated fairly and was in fact being used. I used this to justify the plan I devised: to make things right, I would pocket the profit from one or two jean sales. Who would know, right? Well, the boss knew, and I was promptly out of a job and also realized the foolish thoughts I had were just me trying to justify my own greedy intentions. Even though I wasn't living for God at this point in my life, I knew what was right and wrong. I couldn't blame someone else for my own bad decision. I did not yet have an understanding that sin was beginning to take root in me in that way. Regardless, I had no excuse: I had to open the door and allow sin to enter and take control. It was true then, and it is still true today.

That was me with little, if any, understanding of God's expectations for us. Now if I entertain sin, I not only open the door but I invite it in and treat it like a friend. Why would I or anyone else do something so reckless, knowing the spiritual and often physical consequences of it? The answer is that, whether consciously or subconsciously, we want to do those things sin is trying to enslave us to do. We welcome it to move right in and run things – we romanticize sin. When I say "romanticizing sin," I hope you understand that I mean our flirtation with sin, our having an affair with it. I had to come to this realization that my very nature craved sin. I believe we all have to recognize that in ourselves. James describes it well in James 1:14-15 (NKJV): *"But each one is tempted when he is drawn away by his own desires and enticed. Then when desire has conceived, it gives birth to sin; and sin, when it is full-grown, brings forth death."* Do you see the flirtation? That's our sin nature that draws us, and when we entertain it long enough, we can't help but be entangled in sin.

Getting back to the scripture in Genesis 4:7, God acknowledges that we have this sinful nature, but He does not give us a pass. He still gives us His expectation: "You must master it." Years ago, I walked away from the things of the Lord – I went prodigal, I guess you can say. I began to live life apart from God, and in doing so, I started on a destructive path. I was allowing sin to have its way in me. I was wrong to open the door to sin and allow it to master me, my thoughts, and my actions. I became a slave to sin willfully. For a long time, I just moved on and pretended that giving in to sin was not that big a deal. This was just how life was, and everyone else was doing the same thing anyway. I subconsciously assumed that God understood my bad decisions and it was okay.

What was happening to me was that my heart was becoming hardened, and sin became a part of life as usual. No repentance, no confession, I just continued on with life. All of this continued until God got ahold of my heart and showed me that every time I chose to sin, it was an offense to Him, and it *was* a big deal. I then understood that I could not just continue to let sin reign in me unchecked. Romans 6:12 (NKJV) says, *"Therefore do not let sin reign in your mortal body, that you should obey it in its lusts."* There were consequences to living this way. Life wasn't going the way I thought or would have liked. There were ruined relationships, financial uncertainties, and spiritual emptiness. I was broken – I had to evaluate my condition, own up to my bad decisions, and turn back to God.

That is where change started with me, and this is where it needs to begin with you as well. Please understand, you do not have to "go prodigal" as I did to evaluate yourself in this way. That applies to the person who regularly attends church and maybe even serves in some capacity as well. Even today, I have to stay ready and actively watch so that I don't give sin an inch. You have to recognize that though you are saved by God's grace, there is nowhere in scripture that says to continue living a sinful life. You have to take responsibility, confess your sins to God, and repent. It may take a long time to become free from certain sins you have allowed in, but the formula is always the same, not just for your salvation but for your spiritual health: confess and repent. His Word reassures us in 1 John 1:9 (NKJV), *"If we confess our sins, He is faithful and just to forgive us our sins and to cleanse us from all unrighteousness."* If we are children of God, then we are commanded to walk in righteousness.

So, then, it's accurate to say that we can be the accomplice of sin, but we're also the victim. It seems like an oxymoron, but it is true. We are helping the perpetrator to cause us harm, making us the victim as well as his helper. Just think of how it would look to help a robber break into your house and steal your belongings, then help him pack everything up and watch him drive off with all of your things. That's the cruel reality of it, but we don't have to continue to live this way.

We are accountable to God first and foremost, but it helps to be accountable to others as well. We need each other in this walk with Jesus. 1 Thessalonians 5:11 (ESV) says, *"Therefore encourage one another and build one another up, just as you are doing."* I was once told that there are no lone rangers in Christianity, or at least there shouldn't be. This Christian life is too hard to try and walk out on our own. In Jeremiah 17:9 (NKJV), the scripture reads, *"The heart is deceitful above all things, and desperately wicked; who can know it?"* As I discussed earlier, our own nature draws us toward sin, so how can we trust ourselves with it alone? We cannot live in deception thinking we can manage ourselves. We need help, so we need to develop godly relationships with people who are authentic and truly love the Lord. In this way, I can help you through your tough times and you can help me through mine.

The first step I had to take in this process of letting go of this twisted relationship with sin was to admit I was in the wrong and begin taking responsibility for my choices and my actions. If this is where you are today, struggling with sin, then maybe this should be your first step too. After I took responsibility for my actions, I then felt led to understand what righteousness actually was. There are many reasons why we should not allow ourselves to be enticed and drawn away by our sinful desires, but living a righteous life is definitely one of them. I intend to cover that further, but before we go there, let me share with you why righteousness is so important.

# CHAPTER 2 DEVOTIONAL

## SCRIPTURE

Proverbs 28:13 (NKJV)

*"He who covers his sins will not prosper, but whoever confesses and forsakes them will have mercy."*

## DEVOTIONAL

It takes acceptance of responsibility to confess your sin. This may be why people find it difficult to do most of the time. We have to say, "I made that mess, it's all my fault." There is a level of humility that is required for this, and pride can make this very hard to do. It's so refreshing when we come across people who assume responsibility for their actions after making a mistake. It may not be an easy thing to do, but this proverb says it is necessary in order to obtain mercy not only from our fellow man but from the Lord.

## QUESTIONS

Are you one who takes responsibility, or do you find that you cover up? What drives that in you?

_____

_____

_____

_____

What are some ways you can begin taking responsibility for your actions?

_____

_____

_____

_____

*Take time today to confess your sins to God, take responsibility for your actions, and see how God will lift your burdens from you.

# WHAT IS RIGHTEOUSNESS, AND WHY DOES IT MATTER?

What is righteousness? Why is it important to live or walk in righteousness? I once made the mistake of allowing my auto insurance to lapse. In the state where I live, there was a tough penalty for not having your vehicle properly insured. Well, I ended up getting into a minor accident and received a ticket because I could not produce a valid insurance card. The state immediately suspended my license and ordered me to purchase a more costly insurance that I was required to keep for six months.

Until I had proof of this insurance, I was prohibited from driving. I was not in right standing with the law of the land, so I had to pay a penalty for it. Even though I had a vehicle and was able to drive it, I could not legally do so. I lost my privilege, all because I was not obedient to the law. I purchased the mandatory insurance and eventually got my privileges back. I was back in right standing with the law, so I could now legally drive again. This is the basic definition of the word "righteousness."

Biblically, the definition of righteousness is being in right standing with God and His law. God has laws that He expects us to keep. Being obedient to God's law and commands keeps us in good standing before God. That should be the goal that we all aspire to, but the reality is that we are wrapped in this sin nature. No matter how hard we try, there is no possible way you or I can keep God's commandments all the time. What's more discouraging is that the Bible describes our good works this way in Isaiah 64:6 (NKJV): *"But we are all like an unclean thing, and all our righteousnesses are like filthy rags."* How, then, can I walk in righteousness if it's not possible for me to do so?

Before I go into that, I want to talk about how this mentality can lead to spiritual indifference. "If I'm just going to fail anyway, why try?" and "God knows I'm not perfect, so He will just forgive me anyway" are two statements that come to mind. Remember what I said about Genesis 4:7 in chapter 1? God says to Cain that sin is waiting to pounce on him and master him, but he must master it. Since we know that God is not okay with us passively allowing sin to run our lives, we can't allow ourselves to fall into the trap of giving in to our sinful desires. No. God wants us to walk in righteousness, being blameless before Him; this is what allows everyone around us to see that we are His. Look at 1 John 2:29 (NKJV): *"If you know that He is righteous, you know that everyone who practices righteousness is born of Him."* This means that if God is blameless, then you should be a reflection of Him, blameless according to His standards.

So, back to the question: "If it's impossible for me to walk in righteousness, then what am I supposed to do?" If you are asking that question, you have a valid point – in our own power, we cannot ever hope to be righteous before our God. Thankfully, God made a way for us to be righteous. Let's look at 2 Corinthians 5:21 (NASB): *"For our sake he made him to be sin who knew no sin, so that in him we might become the righteousness of God."* The "Him" in this scripture is referring to Jesus Christ, and it says that because of His sacrifice, a transfer is available to us: He will take our unrighteousness and give us His righteousness.

Before God you can now stand righteous, yet not because of anything you have done or even will do.

Remember, the scripture says our good works are as filthy rags before Him. That can be difficult to accept, since we tend to lean toward being performance based. We need to have goals and achieve them in order to measure our successes and importance. However, God's standard for us is unreachable in our own power. We can't do this without His help. Many find this to be unappealing, as it makes them feel weak or inadequate, and they are 100% accurate. But we must push past our pride, which is the root of our trouble accepting the "help" we need from God. We are righteous because Christ made us righteous. So, we live life righteously because of what He did, but we make choices and decisions based on God's righteous law and not our own feelings or desires.

It's like the scripture in 1 John 2:29 mentioned above: people will know that you are His because you live a life in right standing with God. It is because we are called to live righteously that we cannot let sin win, and we definitely cannot be flirting with the enemy. But even knowing that Christ is our righteousness doesn't answer the question of how we are to live righteously, right? When I first started wrestling with this idea of trying to live my life in right standing with God at all times, I was quickly discouraged. I would think that

I was going along well until I slipped up somehow. Maybe I lied to cover up a mistake or said some things that I should not have. Whatever it was, I started to see that I could not live perfectly righteously, and if I had a struggle with sin (and I did), how could I ever be righteous if I was failing so often?

Well, I found that it is a process. There is a religious word used to describe this process, which you may have heard before: sanctification. Sanctification means to be set apart or be made holy. In this process of being made more like Christ, we are maturing or growing. Our responsibility here is to strive to be more like Jesus. We follow Jesus' examples and live our lives in right standing with God as best as we can, knowing that when we stumble, when we miss the mark, His grace and mercy cover us and we can get right back up and keep striving to be like Him. The key is not to allow sin to get a hold of us and cause us to live a life of habitual sin.

I can't see your heart or motives, so I can't say you are sincerely living the best you can to be holy and godly. The only thing I can see is your works, the fruit you produce. I can see those works, and so can the rest of the world. Living a righteous life is sacrificial because there are times when we don't feel spiritual and don't want to do what's right in God's eyes. We live this way because God calls us to it, and also because the rest of the world sees us, so we help to influence their perspective of God. It is selfish for me to live any way I want when I am supposed to be a follower of Christ and the world is watching what I do. I may not be able to see your true motives, but God does see them.

You and I are fooling ourselves when we keep up appearances around certain circles and then live like the devil around others. This is what the Bible refers to as a hypocrite. A hypocrite in biblical days was an actor, many times a street performer. He or she usually wore a mask to put on a show. Remember the story about the young ex-Muslim college student? This is how he viewed the "Christians" around him – proclaiming to be holy but living a compromised life around everyone. They may even have been regular attenders at their local church, possibly even youth leaders. On campus and around their peers, though, their lives did not reflect the righteousness of God. These young men may have believed they were witnessing for Christ, but their witness was tarnished. James 4:7 (NKJV) says, *"Therefore submit to God. Resist the devil and he will flee from you."* This was not a suggestion, it was a mandate. There is personal responsibility that you and I have to take with sin.

There are many scriptures and accounts told in the Bible that I love and that have been helpful to me, but one that has always stuck out to me is the account of Joseph in the book of Genesis. Joseph had many brothers, but he was his father's favorite. As wrong as it was, his father Jacob openly showed favoritism toward his youngest son, which made all of Joseph's brothers despise him. It's a great story, and I really suggest you read it more thoroughly, but for the point I'm making, we'll fast-forward a little. You can find this account in Genesis 39.

Joseph's brothers sold him into slavery, and he ended up working for a high-ranking official named Potiphar. Everything Joseph did was excellent, and God blessed Joseph and all of Potiphar's house because of him. Potiphar put Joseph in charge of all things in his house. Unfortunately, Potiphar had a wife with a wandering eye, and she would stalk Joseph and often try to seduce him. One day, she cornered him and demanded he sleep with her. Instead of giving in to her advances, the Bible says Joseph fled – and he fled with such conviction that as she tried to grab onto his robes, they tore off and he ended up fleeing naked.

The way Joseph reacted to this is the same way we need to respond to sin when it comes calling. Don't play with sin, don't wink at sin, and don't give in to it. Get away from it!

We have to understand our role in our relationship with sin, we have to take responsibility, and we have to understand why we need to remain holy and live a righteous life. I mentioned earlier that we can't do this on our own, and while I found this information to be helpful, I also saw that I needed more help overcoming sin and living a righteous life. Let's look at some ways we can overcome.

# CHAPTER 3 DEVOTIONAL

## SCRIPTURE

Matthew 5:6 (NKJV)

*"Blessed are those who hunger and thirst for righteousness, for they shall be filled."*

## DEVOTIONAL

As hard as we may try, being righteous (just, in right standing) before God is something we can't do. We can give to every charity and help the less fortunate all day every day, and none of it will be enough to be truly righteous. Instead, God gives us His righteousness because nothing else will do. Jesus says that if we go after the things of God with a passion, just as someone who is thirsty will try to find water, He will fill us. Are you looking for God's blessing? Seek to be filled by His righteousness.

## QUESTIONS

How important is it to you to be in right standing before God? Why do you feel that way?

_____

_____

_____

_____

Do you seek after the things of God ahead of everything else? If not, what are some things that you are placing ahead of God in your life?

_____

_____

_____

_____

*Take time today to put all else aside and devote yourself entirely to seeking God in worship and in study.

# How to Overcome

Many years ago, a movie came out about a man who had incredible talents and abilities but was completely unaware of them. This movie was called *The Matrix*. The main character, Neo, was just living his life like any ordinary person. He was stuck in a rut, wanting more out of life, and was searching for something. A character named Morpheus reaches out to him and slowly begins to show Neo who he really is. By the conclusion of the movie, Neo is unstoppable because he has realized who he was and the great power he actually had. He had to realize who he was before this power was awakened in him.

This is also true for you and me. Did you know that you have power and authority? In the movie, the character Neo had this inner power, but this is not reality. We do not have our own inner power – our power and authority belong to our Lord Jesus Christ. I know I keep going back to the beginning, referencing Genesis, but it's important that we understand how we got here. In the beginning, the scripture says we had an unrestricted relationship with God until sin entered the picture. We were free of all corruption; our thoughts and motives were pure. But after sin, we became sin sick. Our thoughts, our speech, our actions became corrupt. We were in bondage now to this sin nature that continuously tries to pull us away from what is righteous and holy. It was impossible for us to reverse this state; we were enslaved.

Scripture says in Romans 6:23 (NKJV), *"For the wages of sin is death, but the gift of God is eternal life in Christ Jesus our Lord."* This scripture says that for serving our sin nature, our payment is death. Thank God it didn't stop there, because it also says that God gave us a gift of eternal life through Jesus Christ. If you are in Christ, those wages that were meant for you are now gone, and instead, you have eternal life. If you are in Christ, you have been bought with a heavy price. We know as Christians that Jesus died on the cross to suffer the death and consequences that were rightfully meant for us. You may be asking, "If I were to die, what other consequences can there be?" If you do have that question, I suggest you check out Matthew 10:28 and see for yourself. That was the price required to redeem us: His death. He lived a righteous, holy, blameless life and suffered the death of a sinner because that's how high the cost was. In exchange for our sin and unrighteousness, Christ gives us His righteousness by which we can enter eternal life.

Since Jesus is the Son of God and He has exchanged His righteousness for ours, we are now truly sons and daughters of God. Look at what scripture says in Romans 8:17 (NIV): *"Now if we are children, then we are heirs – heirs of God and co-heirs with Christ, if indeed we share in his sufferings in order that we may also share in his glory."* Jesus has all power and authority in heaven and on earth. Look at what He says in Luke 10:19-20 (NKJV): *"Behold, I give you the authority to trample on serpents and scorpions, and over all the power of the enemy, and nothing shall by any means hurt you. Nevertheless, do not rejoice in this, that the spirits are subject to you, but rather rejoice because your names are written in heaven."* We have the power and authority over the enemy of our souls. Knowing who you are and whose you are makes a great difference in this fight.

The question I need to ask you now is, who are you? I just explained that in Christ you are now righteous, and you do have authority because He gave it to you. But how do you see yourself? The Word of God says that you are more than a conqueror (Romans 8:37). You also belong to God since He bought you with a high price. You will go from feeling powerless to strong and courageous if you don't forget who you are and whose you are.

I don't know much about horses, but I read once about how a properly trained horse will stay whether he is tied down or not. Just having the lead on is enough for the horse to stay where he is supposed to. When I read that, I saw that when sin has a hold on us, we stay under its control as if we were still enslaved by it. But in fact, Christ broke the very chain of the enemy for us.

As a Christian, you are a joint heir with Christ, but many times we see our brothers and sisters (and ourselves) completely bound by sin – yet if He broke every chain, how can this be? It's perception. The horse in the example above is so trained and used to what to do when on the lead that whether he is tied down or not, he sits patiently as he has been instructed. You and I can be conditioned to believe sin has us bound and chained as before, but scripture teaches us that in Christ we are set free. You are not powerless; maybe you just forgot who you were. The tables turned when you chose to follow Christ. All spiritual enemies must now submit to the name of Jesus Christ in your life. Don't neglect the spiritual authority you have in Christ.

You will need to renounce certain sins that have gained a stronghold in your life. In the book of Ephesians, the apostle Paul writes about putting on the full armor of God so that we can stand against the schemes of the devil. He describes the armor in Ephesians 6:14-17 (NIV): *"Stand firm then, with the belt of truth buckled around your waist, with the breastplate of righteousness in place, and with your feet fitted with the readiness that comes from the gospel of peace. In addition to all this, take up the shield of faith, with which you can extinguish all the flaming arrows of the evil one. Take the helmet of salvation and the sword of the Spirit, which is the word of God."*

This gives us a nice visual of the things necessary to defend ourselves from the attacks of the enemy. The description begins with the belt of truth. Putting on the belt of truth means we walk in truth. The belt kind of holds everything together on the soldier. This is your integrity as a Christian, and it cannot be flimsy – your witness matters. The next piece of armor is the breastplate of righteousness. This piece of armor protects the soldier's most vital organs. This is what was discussed in the last chapter about living a righteous life. It is for your protection to live a righteous life. When you live life outside of the will of God, you leave yourself open to the attacks of an enemy that looks for opportune times to strike. Stay in right standing with God! The next piece of armor is having your feet fitted with readiness. This piece of armor is basically the shoes, and it signifies having solid footing. Your solid footing is the gospel of peace. God's word is your peace, so fill up on His word daily and allow the peace of God to lead you.

Next, the soldier needs to have a shield in order to help defend against the flaming arrows of the enemy. Faith in God and in His word is essential for you as a Christian. Hebrews 11:6 (KJV) says, "But without faith it is impossible to please him: for he that cometh to God must believe that he is, and that he is a rewarder of them that diligently seek him." You will continuously come under the attack of the enemy, and if you are going through life without faith in God or in His promises found in His Word, then you will suffer harm. Faith serves as a shield for you when times get tough, when you feel yourself being pulled by the cares or lustful desires of life. Make no mistake, if you are living for God, the enemy will attack you. You have to be prepared to defend against his fiery darts.

The next piece of armor is the helmet of salvation. The helmet protects the soldier's head in battle. Here is where the battle is most fierce for the believer: the scripture says "For as he thinks in his heart, so is he." (Proverbs 23:7 NKJV), and the enemy of your soul will do all that he can to influence this. Your thoughts normally lead to action, so the kinds of thoughts you are having are critical to your battle with the sin nature.

This is why it does matter what you listen to or what you watch on any type of media. There is a term used in data entry that you may have heard before: "garbage in, garbage out." Consuming filth or provocative content on any platform is dangerous for you because it serves to influence your thoughts and decisions. I used to be one who said I can listen to any type of music I want and it does not influence me in any way. I really believed that; I thought maybe it was a problem for weak-minded or easily influenced people, but not me. Now I look back and see all the opportunities I gave the enemy to plant seeds in my head. The devil looks for any opportunity to get a foothold in your mind, and from there, he will use that as a place to launch attacks and – per his strategy – continue to push you further and further from the things of the Lord.

In the fight against sin in your life, you must protect your mind. The helmet of salvation goes back to remembering who you are. You are saved by God's grace, so you are a child of God. Whatever you once were, you no longer are. 2 Corinthians 5:17 (KJV): *"Therefore if any man be in Christ, he is a new creature: old things are passed away; behold, all things are become new."*

The final piece of armor is the only offensive piece given: the sword of the Spirit. For the soldier, he is able to use the sword to attack his enemy, but also to defend himself. For the Christian, the Word of God can be used in both ways as well. Hebrews 4:12 (NKJV) reads, *"For the word of God is living and powerful, and sharper than any two-edged sword, piercing even to the division of soul and spirit, and of joints and marrow, and is a discerner of the thoughts and intents of the heart."* This has been the Achilles' heel for many a Christian today. When your only exposure to the Word of God is on a Sunday at church or on the radio in your car, you are at a serious disadvantage. Can you picture a soldier of old all armored up and trying to fight his opponent without any weapon in his hand? How do you think that battle will end?

Jesus gave us an example of how to fight the devil in times of temptation. Just go to Matthew 4:1-11, and you will see that with every temptation the devil threw at Jesus, there was a scripture Jesus used to fight him off. Pay close attention to verses 5-7 where the devil quotes (misquotes) scripture to Jesus. You have to know your Word in order to fight off the enemy. If you really want to start experiencing more victory against the sin nature, immerse yourself in God's Word, memorize it, and start using it. Each time the devil tried to tempt Jesus, you see that Jesus used the Word of God to rebut him, until the devil had no recourse but to leave. This was a blueprint given to us to overcome the tempter.

This is a spiritual battle, and you must fight this battle in the Spirit. A strong prayer life is a powerful tool in your battle with the sin nature. As a young man, I had a particularly hard time battling the sin nature, especially with how to handle lust. I really did want to serve the Lord, and I knew that I could not live a life where my lustful desires were controlling me. I was searching for a solution, maybe a how-to book on how to overcome lustful desires in five easy steps.

Unfortunately, this book did not exist, and now, looking back, I don't think it would have been helpful if it did. I realize now that it wasn't that simple.

Prayer was a great help to me in those times. When I was focused on trying to be perfect and following rules, I was really discouraged – it was failure after failure. I see now that when I finally gave it all to the Lord, when I stopped trying to will myself to be a better Christian, that's when I felt the burden start to lift. It took times of prayer; sometimes it was a long prayer, and sometimes it was very short. The amount of time wasn't as important as what I was expressing to God. I felt Him with me more and more. I still had struggles, but it was different this time.

In those days, I had a bout with pornography, which was the worst struggle I had ever encountered. I never had a physical addiction to anything in my life, but when I studied the effects of addiction on people, I noticed some similarities to what I experienced with pornography. It was something I could not break on my own, and it absolutely controlled me. I tried all I knew to do, but I was in over my head. Sin had mastered me and I needed help. At that time, I had no network of believing friends or loved ones. I wanted to serve the Lord, but I was in this bondage, and I was getting close to hopelessness and in danger of falling away from God even further.

One day, I had enough: having no clue how to get free of this, I finally just surrendered it all to the Lord in prayer. It was something I had not done up to that point. After that day of confession, genuine repentance, and sorrowful prayer, I felt something break. God had set me free of the mess I made for myself. This is how I have stayed free from that particular sin for all of these years. I stay close to the Lord by staying in His Word and by having a steady prayer life. He is my strength and my refuge, as His Word says in Psalm 46:1 (NKJV): *"God is our refuge and strength, a very present help in trouble."* He was a very present help at that time, and He remains so in my current life. He will be for you as well if you choose to allow Him in.

I brought those sinful patterns in from the world I grew up in outside of Christ. That lustful sin was something I never learned how to master, and since I did not seek out the help I needed once I came to Christ, it just grew worse and worse. Sin will not be satisfied, it will just require more from you if you continue to entertain it. Sometimes the sin in our lives can seem almost invincible; I felt that way when I was going through this time in my life. I believed that somehow

God could set me free, but I kept feeling like no matter how hard I tried to be "good," I was always going to fail, especially in this area. I was making an idol out of this sin, making it bigger than the promises of God.

If you want to know the real reason why, I will tell you: I secretly wanted to maintain an open door to this sinful desire. When we don't want to deal with the sin in our lives, we will leave a foothold for the enemy of our souls. It is from these areas in our lives that the enemy will use you to inflict hurt, whether to yourself or to others. When the devil left Jesus in the wilderness, the scripture says that he left until there was an opportune time (Luke 4:13). The devil has not changed his playbook – leaving these areas of sin in our lives hidden or repressed will give him the opportunity he needs. The Word says to pray without ceasing (1 Thessalonians 5:17), and that's what it will take to overcome sin in your life.

Since we can make the sin in our lives an idol, we can be agents of the devil. As I wrote above, these territories we refuse to give over to God become a place from which the devil can launch attacks. Just think about it: if you are controlled by your anger, then you can easily hurt other people in a fit of rage. Are you serving God in that scenario? Sadly, you are serving the devil and his purposes. You can apply this to any and every sinful desire you leave unchecked in your life. You are going to have to make a choice, just like Joshua did in the Old Testament: he had to make a stand and tell all of his countrymen to choose who they were going to serve.

If Jesus is truly Lord of your life, then the answer is very clear. If this seems like a gray area, then I just have to remind you of something: "Lord" equals master, not advisor. Jesus is not just your mentor or just a trusted counselor. This is why looking at Jesus as anything other than your King will not work well for you and your spiritual walk. It is why Jesus made this sobering statement in Matthew 7:21 (NKJV), *"Not everyone who says to Me, 'Lord, Lord,' shall enter the kingdom of heaven, but he who does the will of My Father in heaven."* You can't be your own master; that's not what this is. Either He is Lord of all or not Lord at all. If you want to be free from the hold of sin in your life, choose to serve the Lord at all times.

The honest truth is, we don't want to give up control. We confuse stewardship with ownership. Stewardship is managing another's property. You are not your own; one day your life will be done, and you have no control after that. You and I will have to give an account of how we managed this life we were given. We should live our lives that way, knowing we are only stewards of this life. Whatever you don't surrender to the Lord will be a constant problem for you. Choose today who you will serve.

If you are a follower of Jesus Christ, the Bible tells us that we have been set free by what Christ did for us. The Lord has also empowered us to stay free. Acts 1:8 says that you will receive power once the Holy Spirit comes upon you. The Holy Spirit is God's gift to you and me – He abides in us, and the scripture teaches that He will be with us forever. The Greek word used in the Bible for the Holy Spirit is *Paraclete*, which means advocate or helper. He is the power you and I need in order to overcome. You can have many friends, but you will never have one that will stick closer than the Holy Spirit will. In those tough times, in times of struggle, the Holy Spirit is there with you. He will bring God's Word back to mind when you need it most (John 14:26).

I found that overcoming my sin nature was impossible on my own. I imagine many just quit trying altogether because it seems so difficult. I needed some godly friends in my life to stay accountable to, I needed to feed on God's Word daily, and I needed the Holy

Spirit in order to truly overcome. The Holy Spirit is the key to it all; without Him, we are just in our own flesh, just doing the best we can with our own understanding of what's right.

God gives us the stark difference between living in the flesh and walking in the Spirit in Galatians 5:19-24 (NKJV): *"Now the works of the flesh are evident, which are: adultery, fornication, uncleanness, lewdness, idolatry, sorcery, hatred, contentions, jealousies, outbursts of wrath, selfish ambitions, dissentions, heresies, envy, murders, drunkenness, revelries, and the like; of which I tell you beforehand, just as I also told you in time past, that those who practice such things will not inherit the kingdom of God. But the fruit of the Spirit is love, joy, peace, longsuffering, kindness, goodness, faithfulness, gentleness, self-control. Against such there is no law. And those who are Christ's have crucified the flesh with its passions and desires."*

There it is plainly; we have to put the old sin nature to death and embrace the new nature Christ died to give us. If the Holy Spirit lives inside of you, then you have access to and should show evidence of the fruit of the Spirit listed above. You and I cannot master any sin without the power of the Holy Spirit living and operating inside of us. We are able to master sin only by His power, and now we have to maintain that mastery.

The Apostle Paul said in 1 Corinthians 6:12 (NIV), "*"I have the right to do anything, you say – but not everything is beneficial. 'I have the right to do anything' – but I will not be mastered by anything."* Yes, you have freedom in Christ. It is not license, though. You are not given the green light to live any way you want. Anything that can potentially master you and cause you to stumble, stay away from it. Now, how do we maintain mastery over our sin nature?

# CHAPTER 4 DEVOTIONAL

## SCRIPTURE

John 16:33 (NIV)

*"I have told you these things, so that in me you may have peace. In this world you will have trouble. But take heart! I have overcome the world."*

## DEVOTIONAL

I love this scripture. There may be some who are amazed when trouble hits their life, especially when that trouble comes because of their faith in God. But God does not promise us smooth sailing – in fact, He lets us know up front that there will be trouble for us in this world. He has given us His peace for those times in our lives. Jesus is letting us know He has overcome the world that tries to bring you trouble, so don't be afraid, don't let yourself get bent out of shape by it. Give it to Him because He has overcome.

## QUESTIONS

Can you think of anything that is stealing your peace today? How are you managing it?

_____

_____

_____

_____

What can you give over to God today that in Him you can overcome?

_____

_____

_____

_____

*Meditate on His peace today and ask Him to help you overcome the troubles in your life.

# MAINTAINING MASTERY

God does call us to master our sin, and He never changes. We are expected to maintain mastery over our sin at all times, but how can we do this? Since He knew we could not achieve this on our own, He sent His Son, Jesus Christ, to live the life we could not live and satisfy that requirement for us. It is in Christ that we are free of our sin, and it is in Christ that sin is truly mastered. So, when I say "maintaining mastery," I don't mean that it is something you or I can achieve on our own and then live sin-free lives going forward. It may help to look at it like this: Who is master of my life? Is sin running my life, or is God the rightful ruler of my life?

Remember that sin can be very deceptive. You may think that you are in control of your life decisions, but that sin nature, if left unchecked, will usurp or take away your authority. That's exactly what the devil did in the garden back in the book of Genesis: he usurped Man's authority. He had control, and in the same way, the sin nature will take control from you and make you serve it. So, maintaining who is master will dictate who has mastery over your life. As I shared in the previous chapter, this is a spiritual battle, and God has given us powerful spiritual weapons with which to fight.

There are also some practical things I believe are helpful in this constant battle with sin in our lives. Sometimes we look for God to intervene supernaturally in any and all of our life situations, but many times, God's answers to our prayers can be in the practical things. It reminds me of the story I once read about the man who was stuck on his roof in an incredible flood. Someone came along on a rowboat and said, "Come down and get in my rowboat so we can get to safety," but the man replied, "No thanks, I've prayed to God and I have faith that He will rescue me." A while later, another person came by in a motorboat and said the same thing: "Come down and get in the boat so we can get to safety." The man replied the same way: "I've prayed to God and I have faith that He will rescue me." The flood waters were really rising fast at this point and time was running out, but suddenly a helicopter flew to him and the pilot yelled out, "Grab hold of the rope and hold on while I fly you to safety." The man once again replied, "No thanks, I have prayed to God to rescue me and I have faith that He will." So, reluctantly, the pilot flew off. The flood waters continued to rise, and eventually the man drowned. In heaven, he asked God, "I had faith in you, but you didn't save me. Why did you let me die?" God answered, "I sent you a row boat, a motor boat, and a helicopter – what more did you expect?"

When it comes to what we can do practically to fight the sins that we struggle with most, it is easy to make the mistake of thinking that God will make all our struggles disappear in an instant: with a prayer and some huge faith, suddenly you no longer have to deal with your sin struggles. Now, I have seen God deliver people from certain addictions or vices on the spot, but don't be amazed if He doesn't. There is usually a lesson to learn in the journey, and He walks through it with us. The point is that God has some practical things I believe He wants us to do in order to maintain mastery over sin and not allow it to regain mastery over us. Here are a few practical things that I have found useful in this constant fight.

If we have allowed ourselves to get pulled astray by sin, then it is pretty certain we have developed some bad habits. Familiarity is a comforting feeling; we can be familiar with a place like the home or neighborhood we grew up in. We can also be familiar with people, of course, like family, friends, or acquaintances. We tend to gravitate to these people and places, or at least to things that would remind us of them.

This can be a good thing or a bad thing. If you had a positive experience growing up around family and friends, then being around what's familiar can be a good thing. But if those people or places were toxic, then surrounding yourself with that familiarity is bad for you. When I first came to Christ, I had to make a decision to stop doing the things I had done before. I had to choose not to hang around certain friends or acquaintances because I knew that if I did, I would eventually revert back to the things I used to do before I knew Christ.

I knew a man who was like a mentor to me and my friends when we were first starting out in this walk with Christ. We called him Gil, and he'd had a rough life. Gil had been in prison and made many bad choices in his life, but he had found Christ and was a changed man. One of the things he did to protect himself was to stay to himself. He knew that if he got back in the streets, there was a chance he could go back to doing the things that eventually led him to prison. The streets were very familiar to him, but he had to make a decision to stay away.

In my sin struggle, I've had to do the same kind of thing. I developed many bad habits in my youth that I must actively stay away from. Back in grade school, we were not allowed to have candy or gum in class, so we would sneak some in. So long as we kept it hidden from the teacher, there was no problem. We would just hide it in our pockets, our bookbags, or anywhere that it couldn't be easily seen. Seems pretty harmless, right? You probably did the same thing. But this is a good example of a habit you can learn very early in life that can be a problem for you no matter how old you are.

As children, we were constantly being told what to do by everyone from parents to teachers or coaches. So, in order to do what we wanted to do even if it was against the rules, we learned to conceal things. Some of us learned that skill all too well. As an adult, I just carried that same bad habit into careers and relationships. As long as I continued to operate in concealment, I could live a double life. I could keep up appearances and hide my flirtations with secret sins.

The enemy operates in darkness, and he will do what the Word says he does: *"steal and kill and destroy"* (John 10:10 NIV). It's no surprise that we have a tendency to fall back on hiding or concealing our sins – that inclination goes all the way back to Adam and Eve in the garden of Eden. My resolve has been to be more open about things, especially with my spouse. There is no need to have locked phones or multiple social media accounts. Why is all that necessary? Because the enemy operates in darkness. Proverbs 28:1 (NKJV) tells us, *"The wicked flee when no one pursues, but the righteous are bold as a lion."* If you are righteous (in right standing with God), you don't have to run and hide. You can stand boldly, allowing the light of day to reveal that there is nothing wrong that needs to be hidden.

So, break away from things that you know are triggers for you. If you have an alcohol addiction, stay away from places where it's readily available to you. If you have a struggle with lust, don't put yourself in situations where you can be compromised. Did you need an example? If you are dating, don't sleep over at your boyfriend's/girlfriend's place. If you are married, don't go to lunch alone with a co-worker of the opposite sex. Like in the story at the beginning of this chapter, sometimes we hope that God will just make our struggles go away. I do believe He is able to do that, but as I said before, in most cases He is looking for us to put forth effort as well. The man in the flood story just had to step into one of the boats or climb up the rope, but I guess he was looking for a whirlwind to sweep him away to safety. Your safety could be as easy as staying away from those things that entice you toward your secret sin. If you are serious about overcoming sin in your life, start developing new, godly habits.

The church is not meant to be a bunch of people loosely tied to each other. Romans 12:5 (NKJV) says, *"So we, being many, are one body in Christ, and individually members of one another."* Trying to do this by yourself is not a good idea. We need each other, if for no other reason than that we all need accountability. But it's more than that, though. There is a scripture in Amos 3:3 (NKJV) that reads, *"Can two walk together, unless they are agreed?"* The company you keep says a lot about you. This may mean that you have to change the friends you are around currently. If you don't already have someone in your life who can be a mentor to you and can offer you godly wisdom, then I suggest you start your new circle of friends by finding this person. You can control your friend group, so if you have issues with vices, don't hang around with friends who are involved in those vices. It is really a simple choice, but we tend to make our choices based on our carnal desires and not much else. Ask God to send the right people into your life; He is faithful and will put them in your path. I do want to warn you, though, be selective and don't trust just anyone to keep your affairs confidential. The goal is to find someone who you can trust and who is capable of giving you godly wisdom.

Another practical thing that you can do is to keep growing in Christ. Join a Bible study, attend a conference, read books on spiritual growth. Keep pushing forward, striving to be more like Christ each day. If you have a setback, get back up and continue to push forward. There are no breaks in this Christian walk. In fact, if you are not moving forward, then you are drifting backwards. *"Idle hands are the devil's workshop"* (Proverbs 16:27a TLB). Don't be idle in your pursuit of spiritual growth.

It may be that you are not sure what God's plan is for you personally. It is so easy to get stuck on the hamster wheels of life. You are busy as a student getting ready for a profession that will take you places, then you are busy establishing yourself in your new career, and then you may get married and have kids and the business of life will overtake your days. There seems to be no time for anything else. Where does God fit in? How do you have time to deal with the sin nature you struggle with daily?

Believe it or not, you have control over this. It's time to start being intentional. It's time to set aside time in your busy days to seek out the One who made you, the One that can truly free you and keep you free. You must choose today, right now, to do this. This sin nature is something we will have to deal with while we live in this flesh, so it won't just resolve itself, and it's not okay to give into it. Choose to fight, choose obedience, because He requires us to master sin.

I want to make sure that I clearly state this fact: salvation is found in Jesus Christ alone. I can try to live as perfectly as I am capable of, but none of my works will make me holy. Our salvation, our holiness, and our righteousness come from Jesus Christ our Lord. Living my life for my Savior is my reasonable service (Romans 12:1). I saw that in light of God's great mercy and grace, I am compelled to live a life that is pleasing to Him. Not a life that treats sin as a casual thing, but rather a life dedicated to Him.

God is still working on me every single day, and He has brought me a long way from where I was when I first met Him. I haven't reached the top, and I will not in this lifetime – I am not a perfect man, I still miss the mark. It has been a long process, and I have stumbled, I haven't always got it right, but by His grace and the people He has sent into my life, I am in a better place than where I was. Though there have been valleys in this journey, God has blessed me greatly.

I thank God for His many blessings throughout this journey, from a beautiful wife I always say I did not deserve, to pastoral ministry I did not feel equipped to do, to a foster care ministry I didn't feel prepared for. God keeps on opening doors in my life that I wasn't ready for at any other time in my life. It didn't all come at one time, but as I progressed, God would open up something new in His timing. Though I felt I wasn't ready or didn't deserve it, I realize that by His grace, He gave it at the appropriate time. I could not get to this point in life without first addressing the sin nature I was allowing to run unchecked in me.

God once showed me in a dream that He is not willing to wait on me forever to fulfill His purposes in me. He showed me on a run going through the city blocks on a beautiful day. Suddenly, a storm broke out from nowhere, and a funnel cloud appeared and was coming straight for me. I tried to duck into an alley to seek shelter, but there was none. I cried out to Him for His help, and the funnel cloud broke and the day was clear again. The next scene was the continuation of the run. In that dream, that storm was coming for me, and there was nothing that I could do about it except pray for God's help. The feel of the dream was that as I was running, initially it was lackadaisical, purposeless, but after that encounter, the run was with a renewed sense of purpose. I couldn't then – and I can't now – go along, not striving to fulfill His purposes in my life.

Sin is toxic, and though we do struggle and stumble at times, we have to maintain mastery over it by staying in Christ, who is our only way to overcome. I pray that this helps you on your journey to recognize the issues of sin and the urgency you should have to get away from it so that you can fulfill God's purposes in your life.

# CHAPTER 5 DEVOTIONAL

## SCRIPTURE

John 15:4 (NIV)

*"Remain in me, as I also remain in you. No branch can bear fruit by itself; it must remain in the vine. Neither can you bear fruit unless you remain in me."*

## DEVOTIONAL

We desperately need Jesus in this life. Here Jesus shows us that just like the branch relies on the vine (or the root) to be nourished, so we need Jesus. The fruit that He is talking about is what we produce. If we want to produce good fruit, we need to be nourished by our Savior Jesus Christ. Does this scripture mean you can't ever achieve anything in life? No, this scripture is talking about what will last. Whatever you produce in this life that is not done for God will be useless to you in eternity. But even if you attempted to do anything for God in your own strength, it would amount to nothing without Christ. Do you want the things that you do, the things you say, the actions you take to be pleasing to God? Stay rooted in Christ, because only in Him can you do anything that will be pleasing to God.

## QUESTIONS

What are some things you are trying to do in your own strength? How has this been working so far?

_____

_____

_____

_____

What steps can you take to stay close to Christ today?

_____

_____

_____

_____

*Ask the Lord to help you to remain in Him today and every day. Ask Him to help you to bear fruit that is pleasing to the Father.

# Conclusion

I will acknowledge that the visual of openly flirting with sin like a married man may flirt with a strange woman seems extreme and maybe even over the top. God seems to think it is very serious business, though. The bottom line is that we can't live double lives. There is no such thing as straddling a fence – there is no fence. The fence is more like the event horizon of a black hole, which is the point at which you can no longer escape the pull of the black hole. It would take a miracle to survive being caught up by it.

The Bible refers to the "world" in a negative light in 1 John 2:15 (NKJV): *"Do not love the world or the things in the world. If anyone loves the world, the love of the Father is not in him."* The "world" here represents man's autonomous (self-governing) established rulership over this world (which is merely a puppet kingdom for the devil). We live in this world alongside those who have this perspective. Maybe we can call it their worldview – the view that they are the power that runs their own lives, disregarding God as either nonexistent or irrelevant. This world pulls at us because our sin nature resonates with it. If you don't master the sin nature, it will overpower you, and that draw will get stronger and stronger until you are caught up in it. The next thing you know, there is hardly any difference between you and the agnostic neighbor next door. You live a life that is unimpactful for the Kingdom of God. The blessings of God seem to pass you by. You struggle and you can't understand why.

You can't escape the eyes of the Lord; He sees all of our mess, and His Word says that if we continue in our sins, those sins will trap us up eventually (Proverbs 5:21-22). Let me be clear, though: I am not preaching perfectionism here. That is impossible in our own power on this side of Glory. What I am addressing is how casual we can be with what God calls sin. There is a difference between living a lifestyle of sin and just making mistakes or getting it wrong sometimes. I think the best way to explain the difference is with the fruit of the Spirit mentioned in Galatians 5:22-23 (NIV): *"But the fruit of the Spirit is love, joy, peace, forbearance, kindness, goodness, faithfulness, gentleness and self-control. Against such things there is no law."* Take a personal inventory and see if you have these fruits showing up in your life. If your life looks more like the list described in Galatians 5:19-22, then you are probably living a lifestyle that is more influenced by the sin nature than by the Holy Spirit.

There is a big churchy word used in the Bible, "iniquity" – in the Hebrew language, it means to bend, twist, or distort. This is what we do with God's commands when we live lives that are contrary to His will. We can't twist or distort His Word simply to justify our sinful behaviors and lifestyles. Though we make mistakes (and I have made many), God is faithful to pick us up. You will make mistakes, and you will stumble sometimes. That's normal and expected in this life. The Lord Jesus Christ makes mention of what this is like: in His day, there was a custom of washing your feet when you came into a home, since the roads were so dusty and everyone wore sandals. In John 13:8-10 (NKJV), Jesus had an interaction with Peter when He offered to wash the disciples' feet: *"Peter said to Him, 'You shall never wash my feet!' Jesus answered him, 'If I do not wash you, you have no part with Me.' Simon Peter said to Him, 'Lord, not my feet only, but also my hands and my head!' Jesus said to him, 'He who is bathed needs only to wash his feet, but is completely clean; and you are clean, but not all of you.'"*

The good news is that if you are in Christ, then you are already clean. But we are still here in this flesh and on this earth, so as we navigate through life, our feet will get dirty. What this means is that we can't avoid getting messy – it's part of life. Jesus does make us clean, but we have to come to Him to make sure our dirty feet are also cleansed as we walk through this life. I encourage you, as someone who hasn't always gotten it right in the past and who is not perfect, come to the Lord often to get those feet washed.

If you are reading this book and you have never given your life to Christ Jesus, I would like to encourage you to make that decision today. Sin is a destructive thing, and the only way out is through Jesus Christ. You can be made right with God right now. You will have to accept the fact that you are not the owner of your life but a steward. Jesus Christ will now be Lord over your life, but if you do make this decision, He has a Bible full of promises for you, including freedom from sin. It doesn't take any special or magical words that you will need to recite, but confessing with sincerity of heart that Jesus is Lord of your life and believing or putting your full trust in Him (Romans 10:9).

To you who consider yourself to be in Christ or a follower of Jesus, know that a life of sin is unacceptable to Him. If you have been living this life of embracing sin and making it commonplace in your heart and mind, then please consider what I have written about. Why should you continue to leave sin unchecked and open yourself up to the consequences that will come? In Christ, you have all that you need to overcome and be all He has called you to be. It's time to start living it. God has called you for a purpose in this world, to make a difference in it. You can't be effective for Him if you are bogged down by the hold of sin in your life. Be free in Jesus' mighty name!

www.ingramcontent.com/pod-product-compliance
Lightning Source LLC
Chambersburg PA
CBHW071239090426
42736CB00014B/3143